MY CAT HATES THE VET!

MY CAT HATES THE VET!

FOILING FEAR BEFORE, DURING & AFTER VET VISITS

BY

AMY SHOJAI, CABC

A QUICK TIPS GUIDE, VOL. 3

FURRY MUSE

Furry Muse Publishing
Sherman TX 75091-1904

ISBN-10: 1-9444-2315-X
ISBN-13: 978-1-9444-2315-5

PUBLISHER'S NOTE

Every effort has been made to ensure that the information contained in this book is complete and accurate. However, neither the publisher nor the author is engaged in rendering professional advice or services to the individual reader. Further, veterinary medicine and animal behavior science continually evolve. The ideas, procedures, and suggestions contained in this book are not intended as a substitute for consulting with your pet's physician. All matters regarding your pet's health require medical supervision. Neither the author nor the publisher shall be liable or responsible for any loss or damage allegedly arising from any information or suggestion in this book.

The scanning, uploading and distribution of this book via the Internet or via any other means without the permission of the publisher is illegal and punishable by law. Please purchase only authorized electronic editions, and do not participate in or encourage electronic piracy of copyrighted materials. Your support of the author's rights is appreciated.

Publisher: Furry Muse Publishing
               PO Box 1904
               Sherman TX 75091-1904

TABLE OF CONTENTS

DEAR CAT LOVER,

After writing 30+ pet behavior, vet care and training books, preserving "the bond" remains paws-down the most important goal of my career.

Preserving the pet-owner bond is why I wrote my quick-tips guide series. The cat behavior advice is easy to do, and will help your "pet love" grow as your family grows.

You can find lots more free cat-centric advice by subscribing to my Bling, Bitches & Blood Blog at http://amyshojai.com. You can also subscribe to the free Pet Peeves newsletter and my ASK AMY YouTube. Stay tuned for some upcoming feline-tastic care and behavior webinars! Find my books here.

I love hearing what kind of furry info-tainment readers love best—yes, I do answer email! Please write me at amy@shojai.com. Or find me on Twitter (@amyshojai) as well as on Facebook. And now—read on for paw-some step by step tips and more to help relieve your kitty's vet visit angst.

Purrs,

MY CAT HATES THE VET!

My cat Seren-Kitty hates visiting the veterinarian. Sadly, she's not alone, and at her age, she really NEEDS to be seen frequently to keep her purring along.

Nothing against the vet, he's marvelous and is the first practitioner who has managed to give Seren any semblance of a thorough exam in years, No, my little six-pound dynamo simply prefers to stay home. Many cats are home-bodies and love the status quo and turn into kitty-maniacs at the first sniff of change. That's sort of a cat "rule" but (shhhh!) there are ways to change things for the better.

Karma-Kat, my younger teddy-bear-of-a-cat, is more easy-going. But even he becomes a bit shy when outside of his familiar home.

Of course, all cats need veterinary checkups on a routine basis. Seren's 21st birthday is February 1st, 2017, and for these golden oldie kitties, it's even more important they receive regular health checks.

Whatever your cat's age, proper veterinary care is vital to his or her wellbeing. Yet many pet parents delay or avoid taking their beloved felines to the vet for even routine care, because, frankly, they hate putting the cat through the fear, anxiety and stress. I'll admit it—I hate taking Seren for a checkup almost as much as she dislikes the experience.

Maybe your cats disappear when the carriers comes out, or turn into devil-creatures when handled by strangers. Believe me, your cats don't want to bite and scratch you or the veterinary staff. But when they're scared, all bets are off. Nobody can think straight when in terror mode.

And oh, the embarrassment for YOU! Does the veterinary staff wince and get out the welding gloves when you bring "BAD CAT" into the clinic? Is your cat's file marked with red warning notes? That's a common occurrence—but again, the times are a-changing, so read on.

BUT KITTY DOESN'T ACT SICK...

Cats hide illness incredibly well. That's an instinctive defense mechanism to protect them from predators. Cats mask their vulnerability from humans, too, so we easily overlook and delay a wellness check until an issue becomes serious.

Maybe you hate the caterwauling complaints while traveling to the vet. If you have more than one cat, the ones left behind also make their upset feelings known when the treated cat returns. What's up with that?

Set aside for a moment the angst that you and the veterinary staff feel. Your cat's stress levels are even more important. Stress can aggravate or predispose to some kinds of health issues, make sick cats sicker, and delay healing in recovering cats. Stress can even falsify health test results.

My Seren-Kitty Scare

When she was about seven years old, I scheduled Seren's exam to include a dental cleaning and baseline blood work. She didn't seem sick, and her teeth looked fine, but I wanted to establish what her "normal" results were so that in the future we'd recognize changes. I wanted to be a good pet parent.

The veterinarian surprised me with the news that Seren's blood tests indicated problems, and a follow up urinalysis indicated diabetes. A staff member handed me a "cat grabber" net-like restraint tool, and asked me to retrieve her from the holding cage. Seren was so upset they couldn't handle her. Heck, seeing that netting coming at me would've scared the pee out of me, too! And no, I didn't use it to get her.

The following week at home, monitoring Seren's status proved what the veterinarian suspected: Seren's fear and upset had skewed the test results to show a false positive.

Before this, I'd really liked my veterinarian even though the clinic primarily dealt with dogs and horses. Seren's experienced brought home to me just how cat UN-friendly the situation was, and how cats like Seren suffered the consequences. My current veterinarian and staff better understands and cares for cats on their own terms.

Pets Deserve Fear Free Care

In the two decades since Seren adopted us, veterinary medicine has made it possible for Seren to live a long, healthy life. Today, new programs help veterinarians learn new ways to handle and treat cats to make the experience less stressful.

That reduces the "dread factor" for your cat, and you. And in turn, fear free gets kitty more timely health care. What a purr-fectly sensible approach!

Oh, how I wish Seren had these options earlier in life! But even though there are no "feline only" practices in my neck of the woods, veterinarians and staff still can make a huge difference to make the vet visit more pleasant for your cats. So can you.

Reducing and eliminating fear, anxiety and stress while at the veterinary clinic can be accomplished by providing cat-centric facilities, handling, and preparation. That means that pet parents need to offer a "paw" to help their cats before, during and after the visit.

That's win-win for you, the vet staff, and most of all, for your cat. To do that, let's take a look at why cats hate the vet. Only then can we take steps to address the challenges facing our cats, and us as their caretakers.

7 Reasons Cats Hate Vets

Crate Expectations. Cats learn very quickly to recognize cause-and-effect. The appearance of the cat carrier prompts kitty disappearing acts if used only for vet visits.

Car Rides. While humans see out windows and know what's happening, the cats-eye-view from the carrier offers movement without warning. Odd sounds and being in a strange environment raises cat blood pressure and might even prompt motion sickness.

Scary Smells. Cats experience life through their nose. The unfamiliar scent of the hospital—antiseptic, strangers, other animals—can ramp up kitty fright factor. Then when your cat returns home, the odd clinic smells cling to his fur and can make it hard for feline buddies to welcome him home.

Strange Pets. Nothing turns cats into hiss-terical claw-monsters like barking dogs or meowing stranger cats. When confined inside the carrier, your frightened cat can't flee, so the fight-or-flight instinct leaves few options. She may redirect her fear aggression on the nearest target—you, or the vet staff.

Cold Table. While cats may hate getting into the carrier, being dumped on a cold, slick metal table elevates the "strangeness" of the experience. After all, Kitty-Boy's preferred lounging spots are the windowsill with a view, the soft top of the sofa, or a table underneath a warm lamp.

Weird People. The vet and clinic staff love animals, but to your cat, they're from Mars. Maybe they wear uniforms and smell like dogs (spit!), and don't ask permission to pet. The cat might be handled by several different strangers who stink of other pets' fear—the vet tech for temperature or stool sample, for example, and later the veterinarian.

Rude Handling. Having a cold thermometer inserted into kitty nether regions is no way to make friends. Needle sticks for vaccinations aren't much fun, either, but are necessary. The veterinarian and staff often need to hurry the exam along. Cats want and need to be romanced and wooed to gift us with their affection.

Cats remember discomfort, fear, and bad experiences from a veterinary visit and expect them in the future. But they also remember GOOD experiences and anticipate accordingly. Therefore, it's up to us to create positive experiences before, during and after the veterinary visit.

You can do this! Read on to learn more about foiling feline fear, creating positive crate expectations, and turning vet visits into purr-fests. I promise, your cats will thank you.

Stranger Danger!

The Truth Behind "Scaredy Cats"

Cats come by "stranger danger" naturally. They evolved to be suspicious of anything new or different. For a wild creature, such caution kept kitty alive so she avoided potential threats like a weird creature or new situation.

Cats that ignored caution could be eaten—and taken out of the gene pool. Today, kitty caution is a normal part of the adult feline personality. While there are exceptions (kittens often are clueless) most adult cats need time and proper introductions to accept anything new.

Any change of routine can threaten a pets' sense of security. Scaredy cats react with fear to unfamiliar people, places or situations, because they assume the worst. Many kittens are clueless but as the cat matures, this "stranger danger" behavior protects kitties so they don't walk up to hungry critters, dogs or people. A vet visit delivers a triple-whammy by changing the cat's routine, environment, and exposure to strangers.

Cats identify friends by smell. But if they haven't cheek-rubbed, groomed or slept together, strangers "smell funny" and therefore are suspect. Kitties only used to women may fear male veterinarians with lower voices or with beards, for example.

A strange environment like the vet clinic or the car turns up kitty nerves because the boogyman might lurk in some unknown spot. Scary sounds, sights and smells make cats even more scared. Your cat won't know the escape routes or safety zones, so fear becomes the default emotion. Frightened cats either freeze, or defend themselves.

Fearful cats that can't run away may use aggression to protect themselves from perceived danger. A panic attack shuts down the brain so that the cat literally can't think and instinctive fight-or-flight takes over.

While a normal dose of caution keeps cats from becoming coyote kibble, extreme fear makes cats miserable and disrupts your happy home. Constant anxiety increases stress that can make cats sick.

For instance, stress can aggravate bladder inflammation (cystitis), which in turn prompts hit-or-miss bathroom behaviors. Even when the bladder doesn't hurt, anxious cats use potty deposits or will increase scratching behavior as a way to calm themselves—sort of the way nervous humans bite their fingernails.

Scared cats quickly learn that aggressive behavior makes the scary "thing" go away. They use it repeatedly to warn off strangers, for example. Affected cats may turn from offense to defense and back again during the arousal.

They display a mix of defensive body signals (ears flattened sideways, tail tucked, crouching, and leaning away) and aggressive signals (fluffed fur, showing teeth, hissing, growling, swatting, biting, and scratching). Usually, the pupils of their eyes dilate wide with no relation to the amount of light present.

Aggression that arises from fear can make pet parents reluctant to take cats to the vet. And it can make the veterinary staff reluctant to handle your kitty, too. By recognizing the signs of fear aggression, and following a few tips, you can help your cat feel less frightened and more confident. That makes it easy for the vet staff to agree just how special your cat really is.

FOILING FEAR:
BEFORE THE VET VISIT

Helping cats become well-adjusted, tolerant "Christopher Columbus" cats won't happen overnight. Begin during kittenhood for the best result. But many adult cats also show an incredible positive change in c'attitude simply by following these tips.

12 Ways To Soothe Fear Aggression

If the cat's fear aggression is mild and you can avoid the triggers that make your kitty aggress, no other treatment may be necessary. These tips can help diffuse the fear, and you can use these at home. So can your vet, in the clinic itself.

1. **Socialize Kittens.** The prime socialization period for kittens is two-to-seven weeks of age. When you first adopt your kitten, expose youngsters to happy, positive experiences with a

variety of strangers, locations and other pets. That helps them learn that other people, places, and critters can be fun and not scary. For example, take your kitten to visit and be handled by the staff at the veterinary clinic so their only experience isn't a scary needle stick.

2. **Determine Distance Issues.** For shy or aggressive cats, figure out tolerance levels and reactive distance. For instance, kitty may be fine as long as the 'scary person/animal' stays six feet away, but reacts with fear at five feet. Avoid situations by maintaining an appropriate distance between the fearful cat and potential triggers. In the vet clinic situation, that can mean moving holding cages further apart, for example, to keep strange animals a safer distance away.

3. **Give Them Privacy.** Increase the numbers of quiet areas and hiding spots. Elevated perches such as shelf space and small boxes or even cat carriers to hide in make cats feel more secure. At home, that can include adding cat trees, clearing book shelves for perches or offering cat tunnels or empty paper bags for playtime or hiding fun. At the clinic, cats feel happier and more confident when housed in elevated cages than on lower levels.

4. **Don't Stare.** To a little cat, humans look imposing especially when we stare, follow, and try to pet them. Just think of that giant-size hand coming down toward your head! Instead, sit on the floor, and ignore the cat—no eye contact which can be intimidating—and lure the kitten or cat with treats or a toy. Let the cat approach and control the interaction.

5. **Provide Enrichment.** At home, create a house of plenty by providing lots of toys, scratching posts, and litter boxes (at least one per cat, plus one) to reduce competition with other cats. Offer kitty viewing fun by setting up bird baths and squirrel feeders outside windows.

6. **Reduce Stimulation.** Visual contact heightens cat arousal and can increase aggressive episodes or make them worse. So separate cats with solid doors to calm the angst. In the clinic situation, keeping cats out of eye contact with each other (or *spit!* strange dogs) helps lower stress. Cover cage doors with towels to hide upsetting views.

7. **Give Them Calming Scent.** Use of cat pheromone products both at home and in clinic situations ease stress in the cat's territory and/or relationships.

8. **Provide Soothing Sounds.** Music therapy works incredibly well to calm kitty stress. New age sounds, classical music, and tempos that mimic a resting heartbeat speed help enormously. Harp music is a natural sedative for which you need no prescription. Some music today has been designed specifically with cats in mind.

9. **Offer Natural Help.** Rescue Remedy or similar products can help shy and fearful pets. We're not sure how these vibrational therapies really work. Some professionals suspect the placebo effect influences how well they work but—if it reduces kitty stress, I'm all for placebo effect!

10. **Use Play Therapy.** Interactive play builds feline confidence. I like fishing pole style toys the cat gets to chase and catch. A favorite game or toy

can be a familiar comfort, and normalize the clinic visit, even when in the hands of the veterinary nurse during the visit. When cats engage in fun games, their brains can't be happy and scared at the same time. A long distance interactive toy like fishing-pole lures teach cats you are fun to be around, but without having to get too close. You can even sit on top of the bed, and "tease" the cat that hides underneath without scaring the kitty by reaching under to grab him.

11. **Offer Treats.** If your cat loves food, offer smelly treats to diffuse the angst. Have vet staff drop or toss treats when they arrive at the exam room door, so their entry signals "food" instead of "stranger danger."

12. **Teach Tricks.** Training cats to do tricks builds confidence and helps improve the bond you share. You can use clicker training to communicate with your cat, and associate positive things (treats, toys, attention) with otherwise angst-causing situations like vet visits, car rides or crate training.

KITTY CRATE TRAINING

Why would you want to "cage" your cat and put him in kitty jail? Isn't that mean?

Actually, it's not cruel, but without proper introduction, it can be a wee bit scary. In my Complete Kitten Care book, I call this *LIBERATION TRAINING*. Teaching your new cat to accept the kitty carrier is a safety issue, but also means they get a ticket to ride…and travel beyond the confines of your house and yard, to visit Grandma's house and the vet.

That doesn't mean your cat automatically understands the concept, though, so this section not only explains the benefits of crate training to YOU, it also helps you purr-suade your cats that the notion is a CRATE IDEA. Sorry, couldn't resist. ☺

Benefits Of Carriers

Most kittens–and even their adult counterparts–feel more secure in a small, enclosed den-like area. It's easiest to introduce young cats but felines of any age can be taught that a carrier is a very-good-cat-spot.

Prime Nap Spot. A crate works well as a bed. When a pet claims the spot for naps, it's no longer scary, but becomes a happy, familiar place he feels secure.

Private Retreat. Because it's enclosed, the kitty carrier also serves as a safe retreat to get away from other pets or pestering children. Don't you want a private place of your own where you won't be bothered? Cats are no different.

Safe Confinement. A crate also can be the safest place to confine your precious cat to keep him from pottying in the wrong spot or scaling the drapes or doorway dashing when you can't watch him. A carrier protects and confines cats during car travel, too, such as visits to and from the vet. Some carriers undergo safety crash tests for extra peace of mind.

Ideal Travel Buddy. All pets need to travel by car to the veterinarian from time to time. That's a STRANGER DANGER moment especially for cats, so already feeling safe and comfy in a familiar carrier puts at ease at the vet.

How To Choose The Best Crate

The perfect crate or carrier should be just large enough for a pet to go inside, turn around, and lie down to sleep. It can be a solid hard plastic container, wire mesh cage or soft-sided duffle-type carrier. Of course, kittens grow, so take into account your cat's future adult size before investing in a pricy carrier.

Put yourself in your cat's "paws" to help choose the best carrier. How would you feel about having a stranger's huge hands (as big as your whole body!) reach into your personal space, grab and drag you out of a cozy bed? Associating the carrier with that scary experience means Kitty hides the next time it makes an appearance.

The best crates and carriers have a couple of openings for the cat to go in and out without being forced. Look for those that have both a side and a top easy access opening. Instead of forcing him into or dragging him out of the carrier, you can simply lift away part of the enclosure. The vet may be able to perform an exam while the cat never leaves the comfort of his bed.

Some of the hard sided crates come apart so that the top simply lifts off the cat. My kitty Seren loves her duffle-style soft carrier, which has a padded bed that slides out with her on it.

There are also round carriers which zipper open and close like a clam shell, making access to the cat a breeze and far less angst-inspiring. That's important whether your cats are fearful, or illness and mobility makes them reluctant to move.

8 Tips To Crate Train Pets

The key to training cats to accept the carrier is to create familiarity. You do that by introducing him to this new situation in a series of non-threatening, gradual steps.

If your cat is already fearful of the crate, getting a new one without those old, scary associations may help. Also, ask your veterinarian about medication that may help reduce anxiety or nausea. Some cats hate going to the vet because they get car sick, and scared cats can't learn new things when they are fearful.

Location Is Key. While well-adjusted kittens tend to be curious, some tend toward shyness. Anything new prompts suspicion. So make the crate or carrier "part of the furniture" and set it out in a safe, familiar place like your bedroom or the family room for your cat to explore. It should be convenient for you to access, too, and away from lots of traffic so the cat has a private place to retreat. Leave the top portion of the carrier open or take it off completely, and let him sniff it inside and out. Consider some "second story" locations, so that your cat has the added allure of an elevated lookout. Take a cue from your cat's current favorite hangouts, and offer a location he already loves. Many cats love warm sunny spots, so a window view could be a great location. Don't make a big deal out of it.

Make It A Happy Place. Place a snuggly kitty blanket inside, or even a fuzzy shirt that YOU have worn. That associates the carrier with your familiar and trusted scent. Adding a spritz of a feline facial pheromone product like Feliway also may help. You'll have that same fuzzy scented blanket to spread on the examining table at the vet clinic, too, so your cat isn't shocked by the weird smelling cold metal.

Add A Toy or Game. Toss a toy inside to create positive experiences with the crate. Ping Pong balls are great fun inside the hard crates. Offer a catnip toy to make points with reluctant cats. Lure your cat inside with a chase-the-red-dot laser game, or flick a feather toy in and out and let him catch it, once he's inside. Reserve his favorite toy to use only near or inside the carrier to elevate the benefit of hanging out in the carrier.

Offer A Treat. Many cats respond well to treat rewards. To make the carrier an even better experience, try tossing a few inside for your cat to discover. If he figures out that every now and then, going inside brings a bonus of yummies, the cat will be more likely to explore and figure out the crate is a terrific place. Make sure that the treats you use for crate training are irresistible, and reserve them for this situation only. Once your cat has begun to visit the crate on his own, try offering an occasional high-value meal (like pungent canned food) but only when he's inside.

Teach Him Tolerance. After your cat spends time willingly inside, try shutting the door briefly. Most kitties tolerate the door shut at least as long as they have something to munch. Praise the dickens out of him! He should know that staying calmly inside the crate earns him good things, maybe even a game of chase-the-red-dot. Repeat several times over the next few days, each time letting the cat out after a few minutes.

Extend Crate Time. By the end of the week, you can begin increasing the time the cat spends in the crate. Some cats feel calmer when inside the carrier if you cover it with a towel because this shuts out at least the visual cues that may raise stress. Scent the towel with the Feliway.

Carry Kitty Around. Once your cat feels comfortable in the carrier with the door shut, drop in a couple of treats and then pick up the carrier while he's in it and carry him around. Give him another treat or play a favorite game as soon as you let him out.

Visit The Car. Finally, take him in the carrier out to the car, sit there and talk to him, then bring him back into the house and release him—don't forget to offer the treat. Repeat the car visit several times before you go any further.

This step-by-step plan works, but slow and steady is the name of the game. Plan on several weeks (not days!) so that your cat is prepared well before ending up in the carrier at the vet. Soon, you should be able to take him for car rides in his carrier, without him throwing a fit.

CAR TRAVEL WITH CATS

Our cats can't imagine something that's never happened to them before. Instead, they remember past experiences and believe the same thing will happen again. Because a kitten's first car trips aren't always that pleasant, some cats dread traveling thereafter.

The first ride in the car takes him away from the only family he's ever known. And if the next several rides end up at the veterinarian for scary medical treatments, it's no wonder cats get their tails in a twist over car rides. Although you have no choice but to try and comfort your new pet, when you whine back at the shivering kitten, you've reinforced his idea that a car ride IS horrible.

Instead, help your cats to associate cars with fun, happy experiences instead of just trips to the vet. The process, called desensitization using classical conditioning, takes patience and time, but works whether your kitty acts scared, sick, or just hyper.

9 Tips For Cat Car Travel

Use A Crate. For safety's sake, kittens and cats must ride inside a carrier while in the car. A loose pet becomes a furry projectile in case of an accident. The driver needs to concentrate on the road and traffic, not the bouncy baby on a lap or under the pedals. Even well-behaved cats loose in the car could be injured, because an airbag will crush the crate and pet if on the front seat during an accident. So be sure to crate train the cat before you hit the road.

Let Him Explore. Even though he'll be inside a crate, it's helpful for kitty to experience positive things about the car before you start the engine. Cats are sensitive to environment and territory which is why they prefer staying home in familiar surroundings. So once the cat carrier is securely in the closed car, sit beside your cat and open the carrier door. Allow him to explore if he wants, but don't force it. Make the car familiar by allowing Kitty to cheek rub and spread his scent to claim the car as purr-sonal territory, and he'll feel more relaxed and happy during travels.

Give Him Smell Comfort. Place the cat's bed, blanket, or a towel you've petted him with inside the car on the back seat. That way, his scent is already inside. Spraying Feliway on the towel or car upholstery also may help the cat feel more relaxed.

Sit For A While. While inside the car with your cat, take care that small kittens don't squirm into cubbyholes under the dashboard. Five minutes is long enough. Repeat this five-minute car visit a couple times a day for several days, extending the time whenever the kitty stays calm. Be ready to get the kitty back into safe, non-scary surroundings should he act overwhelmed. You might see fluffed fur, downward turned ears, a flailing tail and hear vocalizations from hisses and growls to yowls of protest. Some cats won't want to leave the carrier, and that's fine. In those cases, keep the carrier covered with a towel, and don't worry about him exploring the car.

Offer A Treat. For confident cats that like exploring in the car, make meal time car time. After he's calm in the car, feed some of his meals in the car for a week, or offer very high-value treats that kitty gets at no other time. If your cat is more motivated by play or catnip, indulge him with favorites during the car times. He should learn that only these good things in life happen when you're near or inside the car.

Add the Crate. You should be combining the crate training with car visits. Once kitty accepts the car as his territory, place him in his carrier, set it on the back seat (away from air bag danger), and start the car. Then turn off the motor and take him out without going anywhere.

Do this three or four times during the day until the cat takes it as a matter of course. Each time, you'll give him lots of play or other rewards once he's released from the crate.

Start The Car. Finally, after you start the car, open the garage door (if that's where your car is), and back the car to the end of the driveway and stop. Do this two or three times in a day, always letting the pet out after you return. If the pet cries or shows stress, you may be moving too fast for him. The garage door is noisy, after all, and the movement of the car feels odd. The process takes forever, but it works.

Increase The Time. Continue increasing the car-time by increments: a trip around the block and then home, then a trip down the street and back, and so on. Cat calming music CDs may also help during the trip. Make every car trip upbeat and positive so the experience makes the cat look forward to the next trip.

Visit The Vet. As mentioned earlier, it's ideal for your cat to have visits to the vet that are FUN and result in playing, petting and treats, with no scary or unpleasant experiences. That prepares kitty for the times when a veterinary exam is necessary.

FOILING FEAR:
DURING THE VET VISIT

Picking The Best Veterinarian

People become veterinarians because they like and care about animals. Your cat deserves to be cared for by a professional that you trust. Every pet needs routine health care, and as Kitty matures, some extra health care may be needed.

Some individual practices or doctors may suit your needs better than others. It's best to choose a veterinarian and practice that is conveniently located, available when you need them, and willing to answer any questions you have. It's important that you get along well with your cat's veterinarian, too. Mutual respect helps ensure your relationship will best benefit your cat's health, over his lifetime.

Veterinary medicine is in constant evolution, with advances made every day. Today, veterinarians can specialize in different areas of pet care, including feline medicine. You may want to look for a veterinarian who specializes in cat care and/or is a *Cat Friendly Practice.* You can find a cats-only practices and learn more about Cat Friendly Practice clinics by contacting the AAFP, which is American Association of Feline Practitioners. (http://www.catvets.com)

One of the best ways to find a veterinarian is to ask people you trust for a recommendation. When your kitten is from a local breeder, a veterinarian may be available who is already familiar with your kitten's relatives. Shelters often have staff veterinarians or shelter clinics that offer services to adopted pets and their owners. Don't forget to ask family and friends who they trust to care for their special cats. Savvy shelters and rescue operations today use some of the same techniques as vet clinics to ensure their facilities and staff are cat friendly.

Ask whether the veterinary practice is AAHA accredited. AAHA stands for American Animal Hospital Association, which was founded more than 80 years ago. It is a voluntary accrediting organization for small animal hospitals in the United States. Only 12-15 percent of animal hospitals have gone through the rigorous and stringent evaluation process to attain this distinction. You can do a search online to find an AAHA-accredited practice at this link: https://www.aaha.org.

Multi-veterinary practices offer a wide range of services all under one roof. You'll likely have one primary care doctor for your cat. At the same time, your pet will benefit from others within the practice who offer specialized care in specific areas. For instance, a board-certified internist offers expertise in diagnosis of certain health problems above and beyond what a general practice veterinarian may be able to provide.

One of the newest certification programs, Fear Free, is open to individuals (veterinarians, vet techs, behaviorists, trainers and other pet professionals). Plans are in the works to certify entire practices by 2018. The guiding principle is to remove the fear-based obstacles that make vet visits an unpleasant experience for you, your pets, and the medical staff. By implementing fear free practices, cats no longer fear vet visits, which eliminates YOUR dread about putting cats through the experience. Happy, calm cats are easier for clinic staff to provide the best care. You can learn more about Fear Free certification at http://www.fearfreepets.com.

In the best of all possible worlds, you'll be able to choose a veterinarian and practice that is Cat Friendly, AAHA-certified, and Fear Free. Don't be shy about asking local practitioners. Your questions may be what inspires them to go the extra paw-step to become certified!

What To Look For In A Vet Clinic

It's a good idea to make an appointment to visit a potential veterinary clinic ahead of time. The doctor's office is a busy place, though, so call to schedule a time when the staff isn't tied up with surgery or appointments. Chat with the office manager, technicians, and the veterinarian when possible, and ask for a brief tour of the facilities. Some things to consider include:

- Is the clinic certified by AAHA, AAFP or Fear Free? Those designations offer peace of mind, with a standard you can trust. Such practices are more likely to have separate waiting rooms for dogs and cats, because that can ease the stress level of your kitty. Ideally, they also have a separate quarantine area to keep ill cats from being near healthy kitties.

- Cat-centric practices may provide bubbling water fountains, play calming music, or display bird houses near examining room windows to help keep cats calm. Rather than cold metal tables, the exam surface may be more kitty-appealing. Find out if you're allowed to stay with your cat during exams, or if furry patients are treated out of sight. And ask how the staff typically handles frightened cats, and what types of restraints (if any) are typically used and under what circumstances.

- Are boarding or grooming facilities available? If you need to go out of town or your Persian requires fur-attention, you may feel much more comfortable leaving Baby in the expert care of the hospital staff they know and like.

- What about emergency and referral services? If the worst happens, you want to have access to life-saving care. Practices often partner with other vet clinics to offer rotating 24-hour emergency services. Veterinarians should always be willing to confer with their colleagues or specialists to find the best care options for your cat.

- Are the hospital's hours convenient, and is the facility located nearby? Many times, veterinary hospitals offer drop-off services in the morning before you go to work. The closer the clinic, the more apt you will be to seek necessary care promptly rather than putting it off for several days until it's more convenient to travel a long distance.

- Is the cost something you can manage? Specialty practices typically cost a bit more than general practice care. Of course, when it comes to your cat's health, cheaper isn't necessarily better. The expertise of the veterinarian and staff should come first.

- Do you like the veterinarian—does s/he like you? Trust is a huge issue, and you must feel comfortable with the person responsible for your pet's care. The veterinarian you choose should be willing to answer your questions in an understandable fashion, without jargon, and without making you feel "funny" for asking. After all, you both want the best for your cat.

A Partnership For Cat Health

The veterinarian is your partner in health care for the lifetime of your cat. In the best of situations, the veterinarian sees Kitty only a couple of times a year.

Meanwhile, you live with him, and that means you know your feline friend better than anybody. You are in the best position to sound the alarm if your pet feels under the weather, and get him to the veterinarian for the proper care. That's a dynamic and effective health care partnership.

Since you live with your cat and know him the best of all, it's up to you to learn what is "normal" behavior and appearance. That way, you'll easily recognize something that's out of the ordinary, so you can get timely help from your veterinarian.

The veterinarian relies on your information about your cat to provide the best care possible. Does he eat well? Play with enthusiasm? Use the litter box regularly, or have intermittent diarrhea where he misses the mark?

Perhaps he pants or wheezes a bit after a game of chase-the-feather. Or maybe Kitty is the healthiest, best-behaved and prime example of kittenhood ever to grace the examining table.

When you take your cat for his veterinary visit, be prepared to answer questions, offer information, and even ask pointed questions of your own. Don't wait to get home to wonder what the doctor meant by something she said—there are *no* stupid questions when it comes to caring for your kitten. Be sure to get all the information you need to make informed decisions about, and properly care for your feline best friend.

FOILING FEAR:
AFTER THE VET VISIT

One of the most common forms of intercat aggression occurs between cats that formerly were best friends. This type of cat attack can be emotionally upsetting to the victim cat as well as the cats' owners. In many instances, the unexpected attack results from redirected aggression when the aggressor lashes out at a surrogate target since the actual target can't be reached.

A common scenario occurs when one cat from the household leaves home to go to the groomer or veterinarian. When the cat returns home, former kitty friends either snub or outright attack the treated feline. It almost appears that the cats don't recognize each other.

Actually, they don't.

Scent Communication Rules

Cats communicate with vocal, visual and scent cues, and the cat's unique scent serves as the ultimate kitty identification tag. When they sleep together, groom each other, or simply rub against one another in passing, cats share scent. Think of this *communal scent* as a sort of color-coded system that identifies them as belonging to the same family.

When a cat visits the veterinarian, he smells weird upon his return. He's been handled by strangers, perhaps bathed or treated with medicines that smell funny, and may even be ill and smell unhealthy. He's wearing a foreign smelly name tag the other cats don't readily recognize. Those "stranger danger" kitties won't let him get close enough to establish his identity.

When the household cats greet the returning cat with hisses, he naturally gets his back up and acts defensive, too. This situation can escalate beyond the posturing, particularly if the ill cat continues to make trips to and from the vet clinic.

Stop After-Vet-Visit Cat Bashing

Confident kitties usually work out their differences in time. But you can speed up the process, and prevent worsening relationships with these tips.

- Try to schedule routine vet visits for your cats at the same time. That way, they all smell similar after being handled by clinic staff.
- When a cat is ill, his body chemistry can make him smell funny and other cats often change their behavior toward him even before the vet visit. Segregate an ill cat from the others, especially if they're treating him poorly. Cat-bashing just raises the stress levels of all involved, and the longer it goes on, the more time it will take to reverse.
- Segregate the kitty returning from the vet in a room alone for at least half a day. That gives him time to self-groom and remove all the icky clinic smell from his fur, which is so offensive to his cat buddies. It also allows the treated cat time to decompress from the stress of the vet visit so he's less on the defensive. All the cats may be more willing to become reacquainted after a cooling off period. Don't rush to re-integrate the kitty to the rest of the clowder. He may need extra time

to get over the vet visit. There's no urgent need to thrust him back with the rest right away.

- Use a hand towel to pet-pet-pet the other household cats. Pay particular attention to the best-friend cat, rubbing the towel against his cheeks. This gathers the best-friend cat's signature scent, which can then be rubbed over the vet-visit cat to help re-establish communal family scent.

- Monitor the first several hours of the cats' interaction. Segregate the treated cat immediately should there be a cat-bashing / hissy incident.

- For some situations it may be helpful to scent all the cats with a strong-smelling pleasant odor that not only makes them alike, but also distracts them from cat-bashing. For instance, rub your hands with the water from canned tuna, and stroke the back of each cat. That should encourage them to self-groom and potentially groom each other, creating a refreshing of the familiar family scent.

THANK YOU FOR READING!

Dear Reader,

I began writing about pets more than twenty years ago—in dog years I should be dead! I hope you enjoyed reading **MY CAT HATES MY VET!** and that it's helped reduce your feline family's fears.

For cat-to-cat angst and a whole lot more feline behavior tips and tricks, find detailed how-to answers in the full length book, **COMPETABILITY: SOLVING BEHAVIOR PROBLEMS IN YOUR MULTI-CAT HOUSEHOLD.**

Many times I hear from readers who share stories about their dogs and cats, and I'd love to hear from you. Maybe YOUR pet's heartwarming story could be published on my blog or even included in a future book. All cats deserve to be famous!

I'd like to ask a big favor—could you please post a review of this book (loved it, hated it) as I'd enjoy your feedback. You may not realize how much influence readers like you have to make or break a book simply by sharing your thoughts in a review. So if you have the time, here's a link to my author page on Amazon where you can find all my books: http://tinyurl.com/m92z83c

Thank you so much for spending your time with me. Now…go pet your pets!

BIO: Amy Shojai, CABC is an IAABC

certified animal behavior consultant and a nationally known authority on pet care. She is the award-winning author of more than 30 cat and dog books and thousands of articles and columns. She served as the Puppies Expert at Puppies.About.com, and the behavior expert at Cats.About.com, and regularly appears on national radio and television including Animal Planet DOGS 101 and CATS 101.

Amy addresses a wide range of fun-to-serious issues in her work, covering training, behavior, health care, and medical topics. She also writes the September Day "Thrillers With Bite" dog viewpoint series featuring a trained Maine Coon cat and German Shepherd service dog.

She and her husband live with Magic the German Shepherd, a twenty-year-old Siamese "wannabe" Seren, and an adolescent kitten Karma (the dog's best friend). Amy can be reached at her website at www.shojai.com where you can subscribe to her PET PEEVES Newsletter and Ask Amy YouTube Channel, like her on Facebook.com/amyshojai.cabc, follow on Twitter @amyshojai, and check out her Bling, Bitches & Blood Blog at AmyShojai.com.

Printed in Great Britain
by Amazon